A Gracious Hot Mess:

Navigating Friendship, Love & Life in NYC

MELISSA MORALES

ISBN: 172048077X
ISBN-13: 978-1720480778

Cover by Joe Boyle

DEDICATION

For my viejo, my dad Rafo. Thanks for all your unconditional love and support. Words cannot express the deep love and gratitude I feel. Thank you for continuing to watch over us.

CONTENTS

Pray & Thanks

PRAY & THANKS

Even though I am not the most religious and very far from been a good example, I want to thank you God because without you I am nothing. You make the sun shine right after the darkest moment, not a second before, not a second later.

Thanks to my lovely and supportive family: Mami, Vane, Juli, Mia, Sayuri & Harumi. You are the battery that keeps my life going. My heart is yours.

To my very few and close friends. You know who you are especially to my girls: Julissa, Allison, Brenda, Jani, Shillem, Waleska & Sally. Thanks for been there in the good, the bad, and the not so glamorous moments.

To my "proof readers": my 2 Georgias, Ari, Raisa, Amy & Karlita. You ladies rock! I am so grateful for your advice and notes.

To all of you who have heard/read my crazy stories and have supported this: thanks for believing in me! This is for every flawed woman that has sold herself short, felt down, has been criticized, doubted herself, felt broken hearted... don't let people, the world or society define you. You are amazing, and nobody can't take that away from you.

Thank you, thank you, thank you!

GROWING UP VS. GROWING OLD

Viviana had just come from work, when she received the notification that the lease of her apartment in Hell's Kitchen was up in 3 months. In addition, her apartment was one of the chosen ones to be renovated in her building. Vivi's household was quite interesting. She and her 2 male roommates came from different backgrounds and had different personalities. She is a funny, clumsy, very dramatic and outspoken Latina who works in fashion. She is … a glamorous hot mess. The guys are more reserved, organized and structured. They all had the option of looking into other apartments in the same building or moving... again. This was the fourth place she had moved in during the 6 years of living in New York. The thought of moving again was quite exhausting. She felt she had finally found a place that was not a transitioning apartment, but a place she could stay longer. After coming home and looking at herself in the bathroom mirror, she saw what appeared to be a light hair in her hair roots. Curious, she looked in closer because her natural hair color just started to show up, and it was dark brown. For her surprise, she had found her first grey hair. She started to freak out because she felt this "discovery" reinforced the inevitable words she had been thinking over and over a few days earlier when she had just turned 33 years old: She was growing old. She heard her roommates talking in the living room and she came out of her room to talk about the email they all received earlier that day.

Matt: "I think I might move back to Berlin."

Vivi: "But why?"

Matt: "I like it here, but Cristina and I will move in together. It's less expensive there."

Vivi: "Oh my God, I am so happy for you! We are going to miss you"

Adam: "Oh, man congrats"

Matt: "Thank you guys. What are you going to do? Are you thinking on staying in this building?"

Vivi: "Well, I would love to stay in this building. Not many places I could afford in NYC that have a pool and a gym. What do you say Adam?"

Adam: "We can... check another apartment in this building?"

Vivi: "Yes, please! The idea of moving again is so painful. I feel like a nomad. Too many bad news today."

Matt: "What do you mean? What else happened?"

Vivi: "What else happened?! I just discovered my first grey hair!!!"

Adam: "Oh no, you are getting old!"

Vivi: "Shut up Adam!!!"

Matt laughed and says "Don't worry Vivi, you still look young. Don't pay attention to Adam. He is just busting your balls."

That same week, Vivian met with Kimberly, Alicia, Brittany, Pepper & Lola for drinks on Friday night. Earlier that week, Lola & Pepper couldn't join the girls for dinner on Vivi's actual birthday date. All girls have different personalities. They decided to try this new bar that Lola recommended. Lola whose real name was Lauren but never used it, is very free-spirited, flirty and very happy. Despite her nickname, Lola is White American. She is a foodie and loves to try new food everywhere she goes, especially in the inexpensive travels she often does with the money she saves. Lola works selling alcohol to bars and restaurants as an Account Manager. She heard of this bar that was known for their herbal inspired mixologist drinks and was trying to see if this could be a potential client.

After Lola asked for the drinks, they cheered for Vivi's birthday. After they cheered, Lola asked Vivi: "How does it feels to turn 33?" Vivi: "Same shit as turning 31 & 32" saying it with a smile on her face "Just that your body, people, and Facebook start to send you reminders that you are no spring chicken" and laughed.

Brittany: "Oh yes, how to forget Facebook?" Brittany is a mixed girl who is very strong and resilient. She is kind of a rebel with a good heart that moved from her hometown in Atlanta, Georgia to NYC under a Broadway's producer assistant position. She lives in the Lower East side with her girlfriend Casey and their Dachshund dog Chips. She has curly hair and dresses in jeans, striped shirts, converse shoes and aviator shades.

Lola, who was the youngest of the group, asked with a curious gesture on her face: "What do you mean?"

Vivi: "Facebook, with the wedding photos"

Right away, Kimberly said: "and the baby pictures"

Kimberly is sarcastic but paused and assertive. She was engaged, but her man left her for another woman. She doesn't get attached easily after what happened. Kimberly is pro women empowerment, practical and loves to read books. She lives in a one-bedroom apartment in the Upper East Side with her white female French bulldog called Ellie.

Pepper said: "Oh, yeah those". Pepper, whose real name is Patricia, but her friends called her that way, was a sous chef. She is tough and takes no bs from nobody. Pepper is skinny, tall, freckled and has long curly red hair and a very pale skin. She loved to dress in leather jackets, jeans, Levi's t-shirts and Adidas sneakers or leather boots.

Vivi: "What the heck? I even have friends that their kids are already teenagers! And here I am, like I can barely take care of myself! Like, how do they do it?"

Alicia: "Darling, I am a gynecologist that brings babies to this world and I still ask myself the same question. They just do it, and all of you will do if you decide to become a mother." Alicia, who is the oldest of the group, and a traveler, works as a gynecologist. She is a very smart and wise Latina. Alicia lives in Bronx with her corgi dog called *Don* Red. She called him like that because even though she was not a drinker, she would allow herself a glass of red wine occasionally. She is into yoga and a healthy lifestyle.

Pepper: "Not me, I decided it already. No kids for me. Mr. Mustache (her cat) and John (her live-in boyfriend) are all the family I want to have... Well, maybe one more cat"

Lola: "How come? Don't tell me you mean that?"

Pepper: "Of course, I mean it and don't give me that look"

Lola: "What look?"

Pepper: "Same judgmental look I receive from John's parents when I tell them the same. It's like they try to convince me that this is just a phase and that I will love that bundle of joy once it's born. It's like my feelings are already second place to this fictional kid that I don't even know or want to have. His mom even dared to tell me last Christmas, because we have the same conversation each holiday, "John has always been a very sweet boy. You wouldn't want him to resent you and loose him when you are older. You know the woman's clock ticks until a certain point, but then any younger woman could have his baby"

Kimberly: "Nooo. She did not say that"

Pepper: "Yes, she did"

Alicia: "What a bitch!"

Lola: "What did you say to that?"

Pepper: "I said: With all the respect to the love I have for your son, I am ignoring this comment, but I ask you to respect the privacy of our relationship and avoid this type of comment. You just went too far"

Brittany: "Well said Pepper"

Vivi: "Yes, that's another reminder! Those cautionary

tales that people around your start saying as you grow older like "you don't want to be too picky because you don't want to die alone" Like, we all die alone!"

Kimberly: "Or, you want to have kids because you don't want to be sick and old and nobody taking care of you. Sure, let me spend 20 years of my life taking care of this kid to see if when they are old they remember about me and pay baack??? If kids were some type of insurance. Isn't it cheaper and more reliable just to pay an insurance? My point is not about kids or marriage but it's just about how some people try to convince you to make all these things not out of love, but out of fear that if you don't do them you will have a tragic end. Nobody wants to get married or have kids out of fear"

Vivian: "Amen to that sister"

Alicia: "But let's stop talking about marriage and kids. For being a group of friends that don't have any of the two, we have spent too much time talking about the subject, so enough for the night and let's be thankful that we have nights like this and we can go home at any time we want"

Lola said: "Bartender, we need another round of drinks!" while leaning to the bar.

TOXIC RELATIONSHIPS

Monica was sitting at her work's desk putting some paperwork together for the meeting she was having with her boss and a client that afternoon. In the previous meeting, the client had requested a certain material which Monica had put in the quotation.

Monica is a Junior Project Manager in a small company. She is a hard worker but a pushover. The nicest person, but she takes things too personal. Monica is beautiful, not only on the outside, but also on the inside. She volunteers to work with the elderly twice a month and lives in Queens with her sister and nephew. Family and work are her priorities. She is Catholic and a Latina.

While in the meeting, her boss suggested the client to use a material that was much cheaper than the one requested by the client. He said to the client "this is a way better material than that one". However, Monica knew very well they had issues in the last two projects with that material brand.

After the meeting and after the client left, Monica approached her boss and said: "Hi Frank. I understand we are trying to decrease costs, but we have been having issues with the material brand that you recommended. The margin of profit is still high if we keep the original requested material. Here's the quotation in case you need it" while extending the quotation to him.

Frank (Monica's boss): "Monica, I said that was the material that it's going to be used, and the issue we were having is because it was not getting applied properly. This is something that we will need to correct for the next project."

Monica: "With all due respect Frank, I did a research after we started to receive the complaints and there are many complaints about the same material. We are not the only ones that are having issue with it."

Frank: "Are you questioning my knowledge? I am the one in charge in this office and I will have the saying in calling the materials. I appreciate your interest in doing your job, but you still have a lot to learn from this industry. As an assistant project manager, material decision is not part of your responsibilities. You only execute and make sure those deadlines get hit. Those other decisions are my responsibility so please stick to yours."

Monica replied: "I didn't mean to come off wrong. Just remind you the issues we are having with this"

Frank: "I think that you should know that you are not the leader but the follower. And as a follower, I expect you

to trust what I say, not say what you think....
Understood?"

Monica replied with a shaky voice and trying to contain her tears: "Understood"

She was not confrontational but then she reacted in her mind with what she would like to say on her arguments with other people and this was one of those times. A dozen ways to answer Frank came up to her mind after he left, but she went back to her desk and texted Vivi:
Do you want to grab dinner tonight? Tough day at work
Vivi texted back: Let me guess... your idiot boss again?
Monica texted: Yeap
Vivi texted: I am having dinner with Alicia, since she is in the neighborhood, but you can definitely join us.
Monica texted: Yes. I just need a break
Vivi texted: We will be at the Peruvian restaurant in midtown West. 7pm works for you or do you want us to move it a little bit later?
Monica texted: No, that's perfect. I am not working late today. I am punching out the time I am supposed to leave.
Vivi texted: Must be bad.

When there were 5 minutes left for Monica to leave the office, Frank passed her some paperwork for her to fill out that night. He did this as she was getting prepared to leave.

Monica replied: "I have dinner plans tonight but I will be able to fill them out in the morning"

Frank replied: "Oh, it's so out of character for you to leave on time. Not good" while nodding his head in disapproval.

She was angry, especially because she knew the paperwork did not have urgency and he leaves on time every single day, while she stays working late on all the projects.

Monica met later with Vivi and Alicia. While having dinner, Monica went over the details of her day, visibly upset.

Vivi said: "¡*Que se vaya a la mierda*! You need to get another job. *Ese tipo* is messing with your mental health and trying to put you down. He is just a grandiose manipulator. I work in fashion which is a pretty cut-throat, and this guy sounds like one of the mean people from my industry. *Nena, tienes que hacer algo*... like ASAP"

Monica: "You know what's the most unbelievable thing? That when he messes up on the projects, I am the one who has to fix them quickly so that the dates of presentation don't get jeopardize, and he can't even acknowledge that! When his father was sick and died and he had to be out of work for 3 weeks, I bended backwards to have all projects completed. Everything got done even when I was the only one at the office."

Vivi: "¡*Exacto*! That's what makes him feel insecure. You really need to do something about it because this relationship is harming you. I know you love your job, but you cannot keep going through this. It's putting your self-esteem down"

Monica: "Honestly, it is. I am starting to doubt myself"

Vivi: "*Sí y eso no es bueno*. That's why he does it"

Monica: "I've even found myself snapping back at him because I am just so angry about the whole situation"

Alicia: "I agree, Monica. You must do something about it"

Vivi: "I had a similar situation but with an ex girl roommate I used to live with when I moved to NYC. I remember she had a boyfriend and she was super passive-aggressive toward me. She loved to embarrassed me or make me feel bad in front of him. At the beginning, I was so naive that I didn't catch on with what was going on. However, when I did, I realized that she was putting me down because she was insecure. She was practically one of the very few friends I had at the time, since this was before I met most of you."

Alicia: "I think we were only acquaintances by then and we were not close yet"

Vivi: "Yes, only you... I stayed attached to living with her because we used to hang out together a lot and I appreciated her friendship. She started to be kind of a bitch here and there, especially after she got the bf. I spoke with her and she apologized, but her actions turned nasty along with her attitude, so I decided to move out."

Monica: "Oh, I didn't know about this roommate you had. You were already living with the guys when I met you"

Vivi: "I started to live with the guys right after that situation with her"

Monica: "Oh, I see"

Alicia: "Most of the girls don't know about this because is a chapter of my life I am not proud of, but you know I was engaged. David my ex-fiancé was super smart, handsome, and I was totally head over heels for him. He was very detailed and supportive with the medicine career. Well, David started to have tiny jealousy outbursts of the guys in my studying group. Little by little, he started treating me bad. He would tell me he was the only guy that was going to be there to support me. Even with that happening, we still moved in together and after a few months, he proposed. Since he apologized with flowers for his previous actions, I fell for it over and over. One day, we had a big argument and barely saw each other in days. I had just passed an important test and we had a Gala at the medicine school. Since he was giving me attitude when I got home and he was drunk, I told him I was going to this event but didn't invite him. Three hours later, my phone started to get blasted with texts that he was throwing my stuff on the street."

Monica: "*¿Y qué hicistes?*"

Alicia: "I remember I chugged the champagne glass I had on my hand and asked a friend, Marissa, to go with me to the apartment."

Monica: "*¿Y qué pasó?*"

Alicia: "What happened was that he had packed all my stuff in trash bags and left them in the hallway of our apartment floor. He also changed the locks of the door"

Monica: "No. ¡*Estás bromeando*!"

Alicia: "Not at all. So, there are many types of toxic relationships. I also hated the person that I turned into. I was walking on eggshells and unhappy. I had also become a toxic person myself. I would also lash at him and nag him with these extensive texts. I was really unhappy with our relationship. I also felt that he wouldn't support me with my career. He would say that he supported me but if I had an accomplishment, instead of congratulating me, he would always downplay it or had something to win one up. So, the point is: don't stay more than you should. When you start doubting yourself, the toxic relationship is not only with the person that is causing it, but with yourself too. Nobody is worth that."

Monica: "Now I feel awful with my silly story when you evidently went through something so much harder."

Alicia: "If you don't start to cut the toxic relationships at this point of your life, you can easily fall into a relationship like the one I had".

Monica: "You are right"

Vivi: "Of course she is right!"

****They all had a small chuckle****

Vivi: "What are you doing when you get home?"

Monica: "Me? I think I'll finish a bottle of wine and chocolates"

Vivi: "So that's how you are coping with the situation?"

Monica: "Tonight, yes. That's my coping method. Plus, it's Friday night."

Next day, Monica woke up very early in the morning and went to her neighborhood coffee store to grab a latte and work in updating her resume. Even though that she usually preferred quiet spaces, somehow seeing people around her helped her to relax this time. While writing her resume and searching companies to send it to, she heard someone called her name. She turned right away, and it was an ex co-worker from her first job.

Ex co-worker: "Monica?"

Monica: "Nancy? Hi. How are you doing?"

Ex co-worker: "Oh, I am doing great. I just moved to this neighborhood"

Monica: "That's so great. I live in the area too"

Ex co-worker: "Amazing, we are neighbors! Let's have a brunch and catch up"

Monica: "Sounds perfect! Is your number still the same?"

Ex co-worker: "Yes it is, and yours?"

Monica: "Yes, still the same."

Ex co-worker: "Fantastic. Let's do next weekend."

Monica: "Perfect"

Vivi went that Saturday with her roommate Adam to ask about available apartment options in their building. They were thinking about getting a 3 bedroom one since they wanted to look for someone to take Matt's spot. After going there, they found out that they would need to do all the application paperwork again. In addition, they were too early in applying since the options were not in the market yet. Vivi was stressing about her living situation because on one hand she really loved living in this place and she was dreading the idea of moving out. On the other hand, she was reached out by an ex coworker telling her that she had recommended her to a brand in London and they were strongly thinking about hiring her. She still had two weeks to find out if the option of moving to London was real before making a decision.

That Saturday, Lola texted the guy that she had been

hooking up with. They met while she was working with one of her tequila accounts at a bar. Initially, she was not that very attracted to him. He was a skinny bearded Jewish guy with long hair that somehow managed to have a belly. He was not her type. She usually liked fancy guys from Finance or business owners that would take her out to dine and would pamper her. However, she had amazing sex with this guy. He had a small penis but somehow managed to always make her climax. They always had the same ritual. He would text her to invite her to watch a movie in his apartment. Then, he would order the same food from the same restaurant. Finally, they would watch the movie and have sex. Lola would always text him later the next week flipping on him because she didn't want to be in that type of relationship. He would answer that he was not looking to have anything serious, but the routine would start again a week later. He did not respond to her text messages. Their last argument over texts seemed like it reached out to its end. In her anxiety of feeling rejected, she texted Vivi to ask if they could meet.

Lola texted: Hi Vivi. What are you doing?

Vivi texted back: Nothing. In my apartment. Just came back from checking apartments in the building with Adam.

Lola texted: Did you have lunch? Want to grab a bite?

Vivi texted: Yes. I am in! I am sooo hungry

Lola texted: Great! Craft bar in an hour?

Vivi texted: Sounds great. See you there!

They met at the restaurant. Lola was wearing her usual casual style: denim shorts, a band T-shirt (this time was a Rolling Stones t-shirt), some jacket & white flat sneakers. Vivi was wearing a printed top, ripped black jeans & perforated leather chunky heels. The top belonged to the brand of a friend of hers that she had been helping on her spare time.

Lola: "Viv! How are you?"

Vivi: "Very good" while they kissed each other in the cheek.

The host approached them and asked if they were ready to be seated.

Lola: "Yes"

The host lead them to one of the seating booths and passed them the menus. Lola always knew what to order in every restaurant. She was kind of a foodie snob, always suggesting the girls what they should try.

Lola: "Their pork scrapple and veal ricotta meatballs are very popular"

Vivi: "Ok. You order one and I will order the other and we will share. Sounds like a plan?"

Lola: "Sounds like a plan"

The waiter approached them: "Ladies, are you ready to order?"

Lola: "Yes, we will have the baked veal ricotta meatballs and the pork scrapple with eggs"

Waiter: "Anything to drink"

Lola: "Yes, 2 mimosas please"

Waiter: "Is that all?"

Lola: "At the moment, yes"

Waiter leaves

Vivi: "Ahhh, you know me"

Lola smiled back and said: "I know my girls"

Vivi: "What about you? What's going on?"

Lola: "Work has been great. Can't complain. Might get another promotion"

Vivi: "Again? Good for you! So, are we celebrating then? Brunch celebration?"

Lola: "Yes, I am very happy about that. My bosses are happy with my work"

Vivi: "You work it girl. I am very happy for you. Truly. You deserve it."

Lola: "Did you do something yesterday?"

Vivi: "I stayed home since I was kind of tired. I was also talking with Monica over the phone. She's having a very tough time at work."

Lola: "But why? She's so great at what she does and one of the hardest workers I know. Is it her boss again?"

Vivi: "Yes but it's taking too much out of her. She deserves better. This work is killing her happiness. Plus, it's a vicious circle. It's not good for her."

Lola: "I hope she can work out the situation... Talking about vicious circle...I think I finally broke up mine with the Bearded guy."

Vivi: "Do you mean with Mr. Tiny Penis?"

The waiter brought the mimosas at that exact moment and the girls looked down trying to contain their laughter.

Once the waiter left, Lola leaned a bit toward the table and in a lower tone said "That tiny penis hits the spot because I've never cum so many times with someone. It's always so hard for me to cum and with him is like magic."

Vivi: "Hahaha. The VG whisperer?" She laughed

Lola: "Don't make fun of it" while laughing

"It's seriously making me crazy. I am always pretty good at managing the situation with guys and not getting involved. But this guy... this guy is something else. It's making me addicted and then I act like crazy. He is not even that cute"

Vivi: "He is not even that cute, but look how he has you. I think that your "Lola" needs a v-intervention."

**** Lola laughed ****

Lola: "The worst part is that I think he is the one dumping me"

Vivi: "Well, it seems like you couldn't break the cycle so he did it for you. You will have to get over it"

Lola: "I know it's just that sex with him is sooo good and

I am not used to cumin"

Vivi: "Well, you will have to get a vibrator or something but you can't leave Miss Vg drive you to relationships based on that. But then again I cannot say anything. We all been there"

The waiter brought the food and Vivi thanked him.

Lola: "Thank you Viv for your advice"

Vivi: "Plus, you didn't even like this guy that much outside the bedroom. Maybe it's better this way."

Lola: "Yes, I know. It's just sucks getting rejected"

Vivi: "Oh, I know! But you will see. Something better will come along"

Vivi: "By the way, talking about vicious cycles, I am looking for a new apartment... again"

Lola: "Again? Why?"

Vivi: "Because my building decided to renovate the entire floor so we can't renovate the lease"

Lola: "Oh, sorry to hear that"

Vivi: "So my vicious cycle is with the NY state housing. It's so expensive to move and it's not even to own but to rent! I am not sure if I want to keep staying in this city. I love NY with all of my heart. It's the best city in the world, but I need to start thinking what's best for me so..."

Lola: "So what? Finish that sentence"

Vivi: "Well, you have to promise not to say anything to the girls because nothing is sure yet, but I am thinking about moving to London."

Lola: "Are you serious? Noooo"

Vivi: "I was told about a brand that is considering me for a position there, but it's just an early conversation"

Lola: "I am going to miss you!"

Vivi: "I don't know if it's going to happen. That's why I am looking at apartments here in NY. I still have to decide what to do"

Lola: "Hopefully, you will end up making the best decision for your own good."

Vivi: "I hope so, but anyways it's too early to tell."

**** They both started to eat ****

Next weekend, Monica and her ex-coworker Nancy decided to meet for brunch at a French restaurant called Maison Kaiser. Monica ordered a quiche and Nancy ordered smoked salmon and sunny side up eggs. Monica was surprised to see Nancy so positive. Certainly not like the Nancy she remembers from a few years ago. She was always a good person, but she was miserable at that time. She was very grumpy and always very exceptional.

Monica: "I am so glad I ran into you. It' s so good to see you. It has been such a long time. You look so happy. What have you been doing?"

Nancy: "I am finally doing what I've always wanted. I am no longer working as a civil engineer. I quit my job and now I am doing interior design and some consulting. Plus, I moved to the apartment I've wanted for 2 years now"

Monica: "I didn't know that was what you really wanted"

Nancy: "Yes! I was so miserable back when we worked together. I didn't have the courage to do what I really wanted until one day, a friend told me about this course that she took, kind of a seminar that made her more assertive and confident. I went there, and it really improved my life. I am a new person."

Monica listened very closely. She was interested in this seminar since she needed to be more assertive and confident herself to be able to deal with her situation at work.

Monica: "What's the cost of the seminar? When is the next one?"

Nancy: "The seminar is free of charge and actually, I will be part of one at end of this week. You should come and give it a try. It's like a community. You will like it"

Monica: "Will definitely give it a try. Let's keep in touch."

SPIRITUALITY

It was the middle of the night when Alicia received a call while she was sleeping. She looked at the phone dreading that it was one of her patients however, she noticed the missed call was from her brother. She got up really worried that something had happened and immediately called back. His daughter had been sick with a severe case of asthma and had stayed at the hospital recently. Her brother answered the phone and told her their mom had a car accident and she was in the intensive care unit. Alicia had to come home as soon as possible. She immediately turned on her computer and bought the first ticket that was leaving at 11am that day. She only had a few hours to pack and get ready. She called the hospital and notified she was going to be out for a few days. Alicia called Vivi and asked her if Don Red (Alicia's corgi) could stay with her for a few days. She was going through the motions automatically but not thinking much about it, besides that she couldn't believe this was happening. She was at the boarding gate of the airport when she ran into one of her acquaintances from church. She was about 60 years old and was always very sweet. She could see that Alicia was stunned and out of it. Alicia had cried in her cab trip all the way to the airport and her eyes were still red.

Church lady: "Alicia?" while touching her in the arm

Alicia: "Oh, hi."

Church lady: "Are you ok? What happened? You don't seem ok."

Alicia: "My mom had a car accident and she is in intensive care. Situation seems pretty bad."

Church lady: "Oh my Lord. Sorry you are going through this."

Alicia: "I don't know. I really don't. I can't lose her."

Church lady: "Where are you sitting?"

Alicia: "Me? Oh, I am sitting in 24E"

Church lady: "Give me your ticket. Let me see if we can sit together. You are visibly affected by this. You can't be alone."

Alicia: "Thank you, but you really don't have to."

Church lady: "No, my child. You are not ok. There's a reason God made us bump into each other during this difficult moment for you."

Alicia: "Thank you" while extending her boarding pass to the lady.

Church lady: "Don't worry about it. You sit here while I

go to the counter."

The lady came back from the counter. She had given up her better seat to someone else and now she was seating next to Alicia on 24D. They boarded the airplane and the lady prayed for Alicia and her mom during the flight."

When Alicia arrived at the hospital and saw her brother, she looked as tired as him. They both had not slept. However, her brother had a more defeated look on his face. It was at that moment, she knew their mom wasn't going to probably make it. They both hugged and started to cry. They both were very close to their mom. Their dad passed away a few years earlier because of a heart attack and their mother was their rock, their strength during that difficult time. Her brother left to go home and get some sleep while Alicia stayed at the hospital. While she was in the hospital, she had learned that her mom was brain death and they were going to disconnect her from the machines. Alicia waited on her brother to arrive to say Good Bye to their mom. Alicia couldn't believe anything that was happening. Everything was happening so fast. She was a doctor and could be very objective. However, this was her mom, her advisor, her everything. The idea of losing her felt like her world just came to pieces. That strong sense of security was completely taken away from her at this moment. She saw her mom and said her good byes. There was a pastor that came and prayed for her and her mom's soul. During the next couple of hours, her mom's body deteriorated and passed away. Alicia hugged her brother while they cried. She believed in God and she knew God had been with them there in that hospital room. Still, she felt angry because she felt her mom was taken so soon. Her mom was her confidant and her best friend. The rational part of her knew this was part of life and she couldn't take the negative path and ask God why this was happening. However, the emotional part of her couldn't contain. She knew in her heart God was there. She had seen it at the airport, at the hospital and on the closeness with her brother during this difficult moment. However, it was just hard to keep her faith while going through this. The next days were more like a haze. Maybe it was a mix of the lack of sleep and barely eating, but she was numb. She had barely answered the text of the girls and from work. This was a moment that she wanted to be alone and just go through this in the quietest way possible, no noise, no cluster... just her and her thoughts.

Back in NYC, Monica met with her ex co-worker Nancy to go to the seminar they had spoken about. When they arrived, people were very sweet and welcoming. They asked Monica a lot of questions about her work and what she wanted to accomplish, and they all seemed really interested. She got caught a little bit off guard since she was not used to people, besides her friends, to be that interested in her. After all, she was in NYC, a city not known for its hospitality. Monica was looking forward to this all week since she wanted to become more assertive and turn around her situation, especially because her birthday was approaching. She had decided that things had to change. Monica was in a bad moment in her life and she was looking for a way out of it. She knew her hard work would pay off one day, but she knew she needed some tools to improve her situation. While in the workshop, Monica found herself standing up and confessing. Monica found herself opening up to the group and being vulnerable without expecting it. At the end, there was a chance to sign up for the next workshop. This one was not free of charge. The organizers of the event were pushing her to sign up, but even though she felt good about the experience she just had, something was not 100% right. After declining the organizers and Nancy's urgings, she said she was going to think about it and went home. The next week, Monica met with Kimberly and Vivi since they were taking her to dinner for her birthday. Monica loved sea food and the girls found a boat restaurant that had delicious oysters. The restaurant was called Grand Banks. It was a nice Summer night out and they all looked lovely. Monica was wearing an emerald maxi dress with a beautiful flower print from Zara and a metallic clutch from MK. This was her favorite dress and it made her feel very elegant and luxurious even though it was not an expensive outfit. Vivi was wearing a cropped top in a vibrant red color she was given at work because of her allowance. That cropped top made her feel sexy. She paired it with a long skirt she had received by a designer in her previous job. Every piece she received at work represented an experience, a face, a friendship or a struggle at work. Therefore, these meant a lot to her. Kimberly was wearing a black & white Calvin Klein dress with length above the knee. She liked to feel appropriate in the corporate world she was part of, but without sacrificing quality and good taste. It was reflected on her clothes. They all had different styles and budgets, yet they looked fashionable and elegant. More importantly, each style represented who they are and connect to how they feel.

Vivi: "Are you excited Monica? 28 years already! ¡*Mija, ya estás vieja*!"

Monica: "¡*Síííí*!! Thank you girls, for bringing me here. ¡*Me encanta este sitio*!"

Vivi: "It's a beautiful and special night!"

They started to order food and drinks. While they were drinking, they started to talk about their previous birthdays and how much they have changed with age. They talked about the goals that they used to have, the ones they have accomplished, and which ones had changed.

Kimberly asked Monica: "And what are your goals for this year?"

Monica: "Definitely, increase my salary and have more confidence in myself."

Vivi: "Glad to hear that!"

Kimberly, who's great at giving professional advice, asked her: "Are you taking steps toward this?"

Monica: "Actually, I am. I am thinking about enrolling in a course. Last week, I went to this seminar that an ex co-worker of mine invited me to. They were very welcoming and nice. You had to sign up for the next seminar at the end of the event, but I said I was going to think about it."

Kimberly asked curiously: "What is this seminar about?"

Monica: "It's for you to be more assertive and get what you want in life. It's more than $500 though, so it's an investment."

Kimberly: "Kind of a self-help?"

Monica: "Well, *más o menos*"

Vivi: "*¿Más o menos*? Have you researched this? Have you looked for the reviews?"

Monica: "No. It was recommended by my ex co-worker and she looked like she is doing better. Her attitude is different."

Vivi: "¡Monicaaaa! Not even I am that naïve! If somebody asks me for $500, believe me I am going to check if it works, and you need to do the same. You cannot use your saved money on something that is not going to work. What if this is a scam or something that is not going to get the results you want?"

Kimberly asked for the name of the organization and they looked at the web page . Everything seemed alright and legit, until they went to a reviews page in another website. Most of the reviews were describing exactly how she felt in the first seminar, however some of the people that had enrolled in the second seminar had a really bad experience. There was a very high amount of concerning comments comparing this organization to a cult. Not only that, but there were details of how they preyed on people with low self-esteem or in vulnerable points of their life. They all looked at each other shocked.

Vivi, to break up the tension, said: "Gurl, you almost end up in a cult. That's fucked up."

Monica: "There goes my self-improvement. Why *esta mierda* always happens to me?"

Kimberly: "You cannot see it that way. Thank God that you saw this and didn't go there. Things will improve, yo'll see. Remember, when things turn dark it's because good things will follow. Don't give up."

Monica: "What do you do when you feel disheartened and you want to give up?"

Kimberly: "First of all, I don't believe in that. I try to distract myself. I read and work out. If I am in that mood, I go to Central Park on a Sunday and jog. Nature helps me to feel connected and think. Those are my best techniques when I feel uneasy. If I need an advice, I speak with a friend I have. She has a gift and her advice always helps me too. She is like a spiritual counselor."

Monica: "Do you mean like a tarot reader?"

Kimberly: "Kind of, but no, I believe you are the only one in charge of your future, but I see her as a guide, a probability. Nothing is written in stone and you are the only one in charge of your future. However, it helps me to talk with her, just to get it out of it my chest."

Monica: "And you Vivi?"

Vivi: "In my case, I set a goal and become obsessed with accomplishing it. I immerse myself until I get it. I think that's how I have been able to deal. Music also helps me. Sometimes I read the bible. I am not going to lie, I used to be a person with a deeper faith and was religious, but things changed a lot since I moved to New York. Not sure why, but I became more jaded. It's not an excuse, but it's just different from when I was back home and went to church every Sunday with mom."

Monica: "In my case, I try to think about decorating a new part of the house or redecorate my room. Still, I have not been able to shake this feeling of dissatisfaction even by doing that."

Kimberly: "You have not been able to fight it because your body is telling you that you deserve better. Until you address the subject and do something about it, its' when you will start feeling better about yourself."

In that moment, the waiter came with the food and another round of drinks.

Vivi: "And now a toast for Monica, who did not end up in a cult and will turn around this new year to become a successful and confident woman that we know she is. ¡Salud!" while she raised her champagne glass.

Kimberly and Monica raised their glasses too and said "¡*Salud*!"

Brittany was taking her dog to the park when this beautiful little girl approached her to pet her dog Chips. This girl had very curly brown hair and big brown eyes like her.

The little girl was happily petting Chips when her mom started to approach them while the dog jumped and licked the little girl hands.

Brittany: "His name is Chips."

Little Girl: "Chips? Like the potato chips?"
Brittany: "Like the chocolate chips"

Little Girl: "Oooohhh. I love chocolate chip cookies!"

Brittany: "Me too!"

The little girl's mom arrived and says: "So Soorry. She goes to anyone that has a dog and just starts to pet the dogs without asking."

Brittany: "Don't worry at all! I used to be exactly like her. I was obsessed with animals."

Mom: "She looooves animals too."

Mom bends and says: "Tiffany, we gotta go. We have to pick up your brother from soccer class."

Little Girl (Tiffany) replies: "Ok. Ok" while she gets up.

Little Girl starts to walk away with her mom while waiving and saying: "Byyyyeeee! Bye Chips!"

Brittany started to wave back. She thought about how much this girl reminded herself as a kid. Brittany always thought she would have kids. Her girlfriend and her had spoken about it, but it was not a priority for them. However, after seeing this little girl something connected inside of her. She knew she wanted to have a kid... She knew she wanted to be a mom.

THE TALK

Kimberly got invited to a date by a doctor that she met in last year's Thanksgiving's gathering at Alicia's house. The gathering was only one month after Kimberly's ex fiancé left her for another woman. She was destroyed at the time, and the girls had tried to get her out of the apartment, but she was too depressed. That day was the first time she left the house to go to a social event. She met him, they had a nice conversation and ended up hooking up. While they were having sex in his car, they destroyed his medicine book which was valued in $300. It was not only until they finished and got up that they realized it. She laughed, but he was mortified at the situation because he would need to repair it to avoid buying a new one. All the girls were so surprised the next day when she told them what had happened, since sleeping with a guy the first night was out of character for Kimberly. She just described it as a rebound and avoided any further details. Kimberly and the doctor went out twice after that. They enjoyed their time together, but it didn't escalate to anything serious. Kimberly thought he was a womanizer and that's why she kept him at distance. He tried to contact her a few times, but she knew he was only after one thing: having sex. He worked a lot of hours and his schedule was kind of hectic at the hospital.

One night, Kimberly was at home and feeling kind of lonely when she texted him and asked what he was up to. He invited her to come to his apartment and sent a taxi to pick her up. They had drinks and talked about work. Things heated up and they started to have sex. They bumped into one of the wine glasses and it broke. She told him "Are we going to keep breaking stuff every time we have sex?"

He laughed in response.

While having sex, the condom broke, and she was ovulating. She told him, but he just kept going.

In the morning, she woke up when his work pager beeped.

She asked him "Do you have to work now?" He answered: "Most likely since I am on call. Let me call first."

Once he was finished with the call, she asked "Can you give me a towel to take a shower?"

He said: "Sure" while going to the room. She was in the bathroom when he came back. He passed her a purple towel and he opened a packet with a pill and handed it to her while telling her: "Take this". To what she replied: "What is this?"

He said: "It's a plan B since you mentioned you are ovulating."

She was stunned and told him "So, is this the good morning ritual when you bring a girl home? A towel,

36

water and a plan B?"

He said "No, these are samples"

She said: "They can be samples, but you would not have them in your house unless you planned on using them, right?"

He rolled his eyes and left. Two months passed since she saw the doctor when he contacted her twice to invite her to his house again. She had been declining his invitations aggressively.

He texted her: I don't understand why you are so angry now. You used to be so fun when I met you and now you are so different. Why do you get so angry when I only want to see you?

She replied: It's not like you just want to see me. You are only inviting me to your house, nowhere else.

He replied: I am inviting you there because tomorrow I work early. I thought we could have drinks at home and have a good time.

She typed: Exactly! It's not a "let's have dinner". It's not a "let's go to the movies". No effort on your side.

He replied: Nevermind. Keep fighting by yourself.

The doctor cut the conversation.

Vivi went to dinner with Alicia, Monica and Kimberly to the seafood restaurant that Pepper had been working at for a month now. It was a small and dimmed light restaurant in the Soho area. They were dying to try it out before, but now that Pepper was working as sous chef, it was the best excuse. The restaurant was known for their fresh Branzino fish which was like butter in your mouth. While talking to each other about their day at work, Monica told the girls about her frustration. They all knew about it, but lately it has been getting worst. She was a very efficient and determined Junior Project Manager that would get it done. A lot of times, she would need to return to work after being already on her way home because an "issue" had presented at the company. The owners of the company were very happy with her work, but the long hours were starting to get a toll on her happiness.

The girls made the reservation for dinner at 9pm so Monica could make it on time.
Alicia asked Monica: "And you with the frown? Let me guess"
Vivi jumped in the conversation and said: "Work"
Monica said "You guessed right. Is it that obvious?"
The all nodded their head and said "Uhum"
Monica in a defeated voice said: "I am not sure guys. I think I am going to quit"
Vivi: "Quit?!"
Kimberly: "Are you sure about that?"
Monica: "I think so... I am trying really hard but it's not

only about the long hours, it's that I am becoming this angry person that is snapping at people and I don't like it."

Alicia: "Have you tried talking to your boss about the situation?"

Monica: "No, I have not. They are trusting me to get it done. I don't want to sound like a complainer."

Alicia: "It's not about complaining, but if you have a good relationship with the owners and they are happy with your job, they might understand and be reasonable with you. You will never know if you don't try. I am not saying to stay in a job that is making your life miserable, but you should at least try to solve the situation before jumping into a decision."

Monica: " You are right. I will talk to them."

Alicia: "Plus, are you financially prepared to quit? I mean, we live in New York. It's pretty expensive."

Monica: "Yes, I have saved some money to be stable for three months."

Vivi jumps in the conversation again and says: "Whaaaatt??!!! You save money? Who has enough to save in New York! So freaking expensive! Hooowww???!!"

Alicia said: "She's being smart. You should not be living paycheck to paycheck. What if you have an emergency?"

Vivi replied: "Oh, I would definitely be screwed. Like big time screwed"

Monica: "You could save if you wanted to"

Vivi: "How?"

Monica: "You know that fancy Starbucks coffee you get every day? I prepare mine at home and bring it to work. Instead of ordering food or delivery, I bring lunch from home. I also only allow myself to go to dinners once every two weeks."

Vivi: "Ok, I will have to make some changes."

Alicia: "Anyways, Monica you need to have a talk with your boss and Vivi, you need to have a talk with a financial advisor."

Monica said: "I will. Thanks Alicia"

Vivi replies: "I know" and turns her head down

Kimberly said: "And I need to have a talk with the doctor"

Monica replied: "What doctor? Something bad happened?"

Kimberly: "No, not that kind of doctor. The doctor I met at Alicia's party"

Vivi: "You mean, the doctor you fucked at Alicia's party?"

Monica: "Ah, the car sex doctor!!!"

Alicia: "Why do you guys have to talk?"

Kimberly: "You know our fling has been going on and off for a few months. Well, I saw him again the other day and after having sex, he gave me a plan B pill"

Vivi: "Well, he is a doctor"

Kimberly: "Yes but the pill was in his house"

Monica: "Oh, I see"

Kimberly: "Exactly, and that had me thinking. Is he having sex with other women?"

Alicia asked: "Are you exclusive? Did you talk to him?"

Kimberly: "No, I have not, and I will not"

Vivi: "You should. You can't keep guessing, plus it's not even safe"

Kimberly: "I know but if this was a serious relationship, I would, but we both know what this is. I have to be practical, so it is what it is."

Vivi: "For fun or not, I still think you should."

Alicia: "I guess all of you need to have some type of talk."

Monica: "And you Alicia?"

Alicia: "Actually, I did have a talk already"

Vivi: "With whom? I did not know you were going out with someone"

Alicia: "No darling, no. The talk was with my landlord."

Vivi laughed

Kimberly: "What happened?"

Alicia: "My house needs to have the oven and the bathroom fixed"

Vivi: "Not your oven! You love to bake."

Alicia: "I was afraid if I started to ask for stuff, he would increase the rent. However, I asked for it in a subtle way and he is having someone come this week to fix it."

Kimberly: "Glad to hear it"

Alicia: "Yes, he was saying that he and his wife love the monthly carrot cakes I bake for them, and that they couldn't miss them in their coffee time."

Vivi: "That's nice"

Alicia: "Who knew giving them cake would pay off."

Brittany had been seriously thinking about babies for a few weeks now, but hadn't told anything to her girlfriend Casey. She loved her girlfriend and was open to her. However, she was scared that Casey didn't feel as strongly and sure about it as she did. They had been 4 years together, so it was not like they would be rushing into something. Her career was not as settled as her girlfriend's, but they were in a comfortable position and financially stable. She decided that before talking to Casey, she wanted to try to learn as much as she could about adoption and other methods to be a mom. For the next couple of months, she gathered a lot of information about artificial insemination, adoption, sperm donors and other similar topics. She thought it was time to have that conversation with her girlfriend.

When Casey arrived from work, Brittany asked her if they could have a talk.

Casey: "Is everything ok?"

Brittany: "Yes, babe. Everything is ok."

Casey: "What's the matter then? You have the face like you are about to shoot a deer."

Brittany: "Everything is fine. I want to talk about a subject that has increasingly become important to me and honestly, I don't know how you will react."

Casey: "What's up babe? Now I am worried."

Brittany: "Honey, what do you think of having a baby?"

Suddenly, Casey's eyes were wide open, and you could see on her face she thought carefully before replying.

Casey: "Are you serious about this? I know you love babies, but this is a huge responsibility and commitment."

Brittany: "I know it is and I have been looking into it and trying to learn as much as I can."

Casey: "And what are you thinking? I mean, do you want us to adopt? Artificial insemination?"

Brittany: "I have been searching and there's something called reciprocal IVF where both partners participate in the pregnancy. One donates her eggs for the fertilization with the donor sperm and the other one carries the pregnancy. I can carry the pregnancy. I want to do this, but I want to do it with you."

Casey: "It sounds like a great idea babe. I want to be part of creating this baby with you, so IVF sounds like a great opportunity to do it. I know how much you want to be pregnant. It's the thing that makes most sense if one of us it's going to be. Plus, you have healthier eating habits than me."

She continued: "However, we might need to move to New Jersey or another area. This apartment is really small for the baby, the dog, you and me... Are you ok with doing that?"

Brittany looked around and said: "Yes, I am ok with that. You are right, we will need more space."

Casey: "And are you also conscious that a kid is for our entire life? How much is going to cost? That she or he might be bullied at school?"

Brittany grabbed Casey's hands: "Babe, babe, I know... The baby will be ok, and we will be ok. We have overcome worst and we are fine, right? The baby will be strong... like us."

Brittany was always the sentimental and impulsive, and Casey was always the rational and conscious one in the relationship. They made a great pair and they would make great parents... Definitely, a home full of love and care.

ONLINE DATING: LOVE'S FRIEND OR FOE?

One day while at work, Vivi's coworker Anne was telling her about a great guy that she had been dating for three months now and that she met online.

Vivi, curious about it, asked Anne "But where did you meet him? On Tinder?"

Anne replied "No, Tinder is more for hook ups. I met Dennis on Bumble bee"

Vivi: "Bumble bee? What is that?"

Anne: "It's an app where the girl has to start the conversation after the match. You must do it before 24 hours are over."

Vivi: "Why 24 hours?"

Anne: "If you don't initiate the conversation after 24 hours, the match disappears."

Vivi: "Oh, so it already has an expiring date?" and laughs.

Anne laughs and replies "Yes, it does, but the guys are more educated and handsome... Why don't you try it?"

Vivi: "I am not sure. I prefer meeting people in a more normal way."

Anne replied: "Do you mean in a bar?"

Vivi shrugged her shoulders in response.

Anne: "Because let's be realistic. We work in fashion. How many straight guys do we meet in this industry?"

Vivi: "Point taken."

Anne: "Try it. You don't lose anything..." Actually, give

me your phone" while extending her hand to Vivi.

Vivi passed her phone to Anne.

Anne: "I will make you an account. If you don't like what you see or don't meet anyone worth it, close it, but at least give it a chance."

Vivi: "Ok"

After a few minutes, Anne hands over the phone back to Vivi and tells her "Use it"

Vivi noticed she had some matches already and they looked pretty cute. After coming home from work, she started to swipe and for her surprise and shock she encounters the profile of someone she knows pretty well: one of her roommates. She immediately froze and swiped left so fast like she could get rid of the fact that he might see her on his options. Then, she immediately gets out of the app. About half hour later and while watching some Netflix she stopped the movie because she heard her roommates talking.

She went out and asked them "Hey, this question might seem random, but have you guys tried an app called Bumble bee? Is it good or is it a duchy app?"

Adam: "I have used it and it's ok. You can find good people to date there. It's not only for hook ups."

Matt: "I have used it too, before meeting Cristina and it's alright."

Vivi: "Actually, I think I saw you there. You gotta close it man, you are out of the market."

Matt responded while laughing: "Really? I have not been connected in months. Last time I connected was before getting back with Cristina."

Adam: "What did you do? Did you swipe right?"
Vivi laughed sarcastically: "Hahaha, no. I swiped left idiot"
Matt: "Well, let us know how it goes."
Vivi: "Oh, I'll definitely will."
Next day, Vivi opened the application again. This time she noticed one of the guys had used his daily use to lengthen the time with her for more than the programmed 24 hours.
Vivi considered this gesture cute so she decided to start the conversation and texted him. They were talking for a few days and decided to meet. Excited about her date, Vivi told her friend Lola & Monica who came to her apartment for some wine & cheese.
Monica replied "I am done with online dating. I am done with dating in general."
Lola & Vivi: "What happened?"
Monica: "You remember Sergio?"
Vivi: "Yes, what happened with him? You never told us, but since you seemed so upset I didn't want to ask."
Monica: "Found out he had a girlfriend in Madrid."

Vivi: "What?"

Monica: "Yes, so all his trips to go "home" to visit his mother, were in fact to visit his girlfriend of 1 year."

Lola: "What? 1 year?!"

Monica: "If it was not because she started to tag him in photos, I would have never known. I think she suspected that he was going out with someone else."

Vivi: "That sucks"

Monica: "But everyone has different experiences. Yours might be different."

Vivi: "I hope so..."

Monica: "Look at Lola. She has been dating the cyclist for a month now and it is going well."

Lola: "Are we still calling him "the cyclist"?"

Monica: "Yes, you know the rule: until you don't introduce him to us, the guy will have nickname."

Vivi: "Other way, it's too hard to remember all the names and keep track" she laughs.

Lola: "Anyways, I am having dinner again with the cyclist this week. We are going to this bar that opened two months ago and I've been wanting to try."

After a night of dinner and drinks, Lola went to the cyclist's apartment. While making out, the "cyclist" started to undress Lola. She laid on the bed while the "cyclist" started to get undressed. Then, he ran his fingers over her body starting from her thighs. Then moving them to her belly and sliding down to her "Lolita". She started to moan and after a few minutes of having the fingers of the "cyclist" inside of her, things got really hot and heavy and they had intercourse. He started to ask her "Do you like it?"

Lola: "Yes!"

The cyclist was increasingly hitting his climax and they were both really into it.

After a few seconds, Lola felt what was a spit on her chest and she got thrown off. Trying not to cut the mood, she said: "Let me ride you" and they switched positions. She started to ride him, and they kissed very passionately. After a few minutes, he is about to cum and asked Lola

Cyclist: "Spit in my mouth"

Lola: "Whaaat?"

Cyclist: "Spit inside my mouth!"

Disoriented she spited inside his mouth and she made a disgusted face while he came.

He tried to go down on her, but she was so thrown off with all the spitting that she just couldn't and told him she was too tired from that day.

Next morning, she decided to flee his apartment and met with Vivi for brunch.

Vivi: "What happened? I thought you were staying over at the cyclist's"

Lola: "Yes, but I ran away."

Vivi: "Why?"

Lola: "He is a freak. He spited me, I spited him. It was a whole spitting shit show"

Vivi: "What do you mean? Did you argue?"

Lola: "No, we were having sex. I felt like I was in a baseball game"

Vivi: "Eww. I mean, sorry. If you are into that, it's between the two of you."

Lola: "I am not! That's why I escaped but he is a sweet guy. He even got me flowers. Maybe I can try it again. It just took me off guard."

The waiter brought 2 glasses of water and Lola drank hers very fast

Vivi: "You better drink all of it so you can replenish your fluids."

*** Lola laughed almost spilling the water she had on her mouth ***

Lola: "Don't get me wrong, I am not against different. Remember, I hooked up with that race car driver." She hooked up with this Daytona race car driver when she was on vacation in Las Vegas.

And she continued: "But that guy was exciting different, not weirdo different."

Vivi: "Well, it seems that's what floats his boat".

After brunch, they were leaving the diner. It was raining outside, and Lola was opening the door.

Lola: "Wish me luck. I have to see him again tonight."

Vivi: "You will not want to forget" while grabbing the umbrella Lola left at her seat. "You might need it tonight."

Lola looked at Vivi with a mortified sad face but wanting to laugh at the same time.

Later that night, while having sex with the "cyclist", Lola felt relieved. So far, he hasn't given her a signal he wanted to spit. She was kissing him passionately to avoid him trying to spit again. When they were both about to cum, she releases her mouth and starts to moan when he again spited on her. This time she couldn't contain herself and she yelled "enough with the spitting! Sorry, I just can't!" She got her clothes and stormed out of his apartment.

Vivi went to her date but surprisingly all the good chemistry that happened during texts, disappeared the instant they met. Conversation went well, but it fell forced and the whole dinner felt awkward. Viviana went home disappointed. When she got home, Adam was at the kitchen preparing himself something to eat. He saw Vivi opening the door and he asked her "What's the matter with you? Why the long face?"

Vivi: "Nothing, just had a date."

Adam: "Was it bad?"

Vivi: "Yeah. No chemistry."

Adam: "That happens. It's common."

Vivi: "I don't get it. We hit it off so well texting and then the moment we met it was just off, and I mean really off. Like nothing. Zero"

Adam: "Don't worry Vivi. You will find a great guy that deserves you. You are an awesome girl."

Vivi: "Thank you Adam. Good night. I'm going to sleep."

Next day, Vivi went to a fashion party for the opening of a new online platform for artists of the NYC art scene. Vivi knew one of the artists and collaborators of the platform, a very cool and stylish girl named Kai. They have met at a party in the Standard Hotel in East Village a few years ago. They kept in contact once they discovered they both worked in fashion. Monica and Pepper joined her at the party. Kai came to say hi to Vivi and explained the concept and the platform of the party. Monica and Pepper had already drinks on their hands, so Vivi went to the bar with Kai to grab some for themselves. Right there, Kai introduced Vivi to this very tall, long hair model that looked like an Adonis. Kai excused herself, since she spotted the editor of an Avant-guard magazine she had been trying to chase for months now to see her work.

Kai said to Vivi and Davon: "Sorry guys, you will excuse

me, but I HAVE TO talk to her."

Davon said: "No worries. We are in great company, right Vivi?"

Vivi was speechless because of the beauty of this handsome man. All she could say was: "I think so"

Davon and Vivi hit it off and talked for half hour when she felt her phone vibrating, and she noticed it was a text from her friends. They have been looking for her and saw her with this guy from a few meters away.

Vivi said to Davon: "Sorry but I left my friends and I have to go back."

Davon: "It's ok. I also have to go and meet some friends from the agency. How about we exchange numbers and grab a drink later this week?"

Vivi: "That sounds like a plan."

Vivi was in shock. Never had a guy, this good looking (or tall) invited her out.

After quite a few texts, they met on a Wednesday evening. When Vivi got to the bar she saw this amazing looking guy who was her date. She considered herself pretty, but she started doubting "Why the heck does this guy that is so much better looking than me, so out of my league, would be into me?" After 15 minutes into the conversation, she knew what it was. He was attracted to her personality. For her surprise, this guy was a sweet boy and they had a good conversation. He told her his ex-girlfriend cheated on him and had devastated him.

Vivi started to wonder how a girl could have cheated on that handsome sweet boy. However, that night they had too many drinks and they had gone back to his apartment. While they were at his apartment, he started to smoke weed and they started to make out. He couldn't get it up and Vivi passed out asleep, so nothing happened besides kisses. In the morning, Vivi woke up a bit disoriented and with a huge headache. Davon gave her a pill for her headache and a glass of water. She took a cab home, since she had to go to work. On her way to work, she texted Monica.

Vivi texted: Guess what? Stayed over at the model's apartment.
Monica texted back: You slut
Vivi replied: Hahaha. Nothing happened. Well, we made out, but nothing else.
Monica texted: Too bad because that guy was a cutie.
Vivi replied: Still, I am happy I can put him on my made-out list
Monica: Do you think you will see him again?
Vivi: No, I don't think so. He is handsome and a good person, but I think it's just a fling.
Monica: Well, at least this one is redemption for the ugly ones you have kissed.
Vivi: Yes, ugly guys are the worst. They make you fall in love with them and when they are jerks, you are like

who do you think you are? You are not even that cute to be a jerk!

Monica: LMAO, so true

Vivi: What are you up to this weekend? I am thinking about cooking pasta and inviting you and Kimberly. I haven't spoken to her in more than 2 weeks, so I thought Saturday night would be a good night to do it.

Monica: I cannot do Saturday, I have a date.

Vivi: Really? You didn't tell me you met someone!

Monica: I have not met him yet.

Vivi: Wait, is this an online date?

Monica: Yes, it is.

Vivi: But I thought you said you were done with online dating? Actually, if I recall well, your words were "I am done with dating in general"

Monica: Yes, you are right, but I decided to give it a second chance after our talk. I found myself becoming too cynical and aggressive toward men.

Vivi: Don't take it too seriously and enjoy.

ARE WE ALL CREEPS OR JUST CAUTIOUS?

Alicia, Vivi and Monica had a picnic while they were assisting to an opera concert at Central Park.

Alicia: "What's new with you Vivi? I have not seen you in forever."

Vivi: "Same thing at work. Well, I do have news. I went on a date with a hottie. Actually, I have a picture here from his Instagram."

Alicia: "Let me see"

Alicia, trying to enlarge the picture, double clicks the photo and likes it by mistake.

Vivi freaks out because the picture it's with another woman. She thinks might be the sister, might be a friend, might be an ex? Oh my God, what if it's an ex and he thinks that I am psycho? Oh no! Let me like another random pic. It would be weird just to hit like in the picture that he is with a woman.

Vivi: "Oh my God, I am going to kill you Alicia!". She says while liking the second picture.

She received a text from this guy immediately after that.

Guy from picture texted: Creeping much?

Vivi told Alicia: "Crap! It's him!!!" While looking perplexed to her cellphone (grabbing phone with both hands)

Alicia: "Who?"

Vivi: "The guy!"

Alicia: "What guy?"

Vivi: "The guuuy!!!!" while shaking her cellphone flashing it to Alicia and showing her the picture she just liked.

Alicia: "Sooo soorryyy. What's he saying?"

Vivi: "He's saying - creeping much? This is so embarrassing. Now he is going to think I am a psycho"

Vivi texted "I am so sorry. I was showing a picture to my friend of the guy I went on a date with and she liked it by mistake. Then, I liked another picture to not look like a creep, but I just made it worst. So sorry. I am going to kill her!"

Guy: "Hahaha, don't. I think it's funny"

Alicia: "What did he say?"

Vivi: "He thinks it's funny" she said with a smirk on her face and in disbelief.

Alicia: "You see, he doesn't think you are a psycho. Why would you think he would?"

Vivi: "Because I've been a psycho"

Monica: "No you have not"

Vivi: "Yes, I have been. I used to drunk-text my booty call late and insist. That's not good. I don't know how he even dealt with me"

Alicia: "One thing...sex"

Vivi: "No, sometimes I would just go there and sleep"

Monica: "You mean like a sleepover?"

Vivi: "Yes"

Alicia: "That's unusual"

Vivi: "I just wanted to sleep and cuddled with him. He would always deal with me. No matter how late. I am not sure why he even did it. I wouldn't have."

Monica: "Maybe he liked you."

Alicia: "Or maybe he likes psychos."

Vivi: " He probably did."

Monica: "Well, I am a psycho too. As soon as I meet a guy, I immediately check all his social media: Facebook, Instagram, you name it."

Alicia: "Why?"

Monica: "Just want to make sure he does not have a girlfriend, or he is not a psycho, or a creep."

Alicia: "Isn't that ironic when you are the one checking his social media?"

Monica: "I guess, but at least he doesn't know that" and laughs.

*** All laughed ***

Kimberly had the suspicion the guy she had dated for six months now, was dating another girl. Even though he would spend a lot of time in her apartment, she felt something was not right. One day, after he left his Instagram open, she had the curiosity of checking his DM (direct messages). Of course, she knew that was not the right thing to do, but she felt a strong nagging feeling and she did it anyways. For her surprise, he was not cheating on her with a girl but with a guy. Their conversations were only through Instagram and there has not been an encounter. Yet, she felt deeply betrayed and disgusted. Not because it was a guy, but because she realized she did not know this person at all. After seeing this, she threw his stuff to the hallway and called him, insulting and telling him to pick up his stuff from the hallway. In the next days, Kimberly submerged herself into her work. She had a project that she had to finalize at work and a deadline for the presentation to her bosses. It was very hard to concentrate while trying to deal with this situation. On her breaks from work, she would read articles about the subject and read books. After her presentation at work, and still traumatized about the whole situation, she asked Vivi and Brittany if they could meet for a coffee. Kimberly told both what happened that night while they were speechless listening to the story.

Kimberly: "Mike was cheating... with a guy. Can you believe it? And, all he kept saying when I confronted him was that nothing happened! I don't care if something happened, for me he cheated anyways. And, with a guy... A guy!!!! I mean, why didn't he say he was bi?!" They were both jaw-dropped speechless. All they could do was nod their heads in disapproval.

Kimberly: "Then, he was in denial and trying to turn it on

me. Like, why was I checking his inbox? Like if I am the psycho or the one that committed the fault here. Can you imagine if I wouldn't have done that? He would be lying, and God knows what else?!"

Vivi: "It's not ok to go through other person's private stuff, but in this case, you did the right thing. At least something positive came out of it"

Kimberly: "Yeah, who knew that being psycho would pay off this time"

Brittany: "Kimberly, sorry to hear that you went through that. Sorry if I don't know what to say about it. It must be hard"

Kimberly: "Yes, because I was not expecting it. Plus, you start to wonder how many times he has done this before. It was pretty scary. I ran to do an STD test after that. I was really lucky it came alright. I was really scared."

Vivi: "That was my first thought when I heard it. Glad to hear you are alright... I mean, not alright because you are really angry, and this is emotionally frustrating for any woman, but it could have been so much worst... Way worst."

Kimberly: "Definitely! I was very worried. While I was waiting for the results, I started to look at the statistics of straight women that get infected with HIV and other STD's from their husbands. Getting infected is more common than you would think."

Brittany: "There's even a slang term for this in the African American community. It's called down-low brothers, and it refers to men that secretly engage in homosexual conduct, but live a heterosexual lifestyle. A lot of men that are still in the closet, marry a woman and have a family too. Then, they cheat on their wives with men. Sexual preference is not a decision, we are born with it. However, I can't understand why people think they can put it on hold or think they can change. It's an elusive thinking. We cannot change who we are. I am a lesbian and come from a very religious home. It was hard to come out to my parents, but I would have never even considered living a lie like this. It's a life full of deception."

Vivi: "Brittany, how was it when you came out to your parents?"

Brittany: "It was a very difficult situation. I felt like my mom always knew, so I came out to her first when I was in high school. I had this girlfriend that would come home after school very often. My mom walked one day into my room and caught us kissing. I came out to her, but asked her not to tell my dad. After moving to New York, which he disapproved because he thought I was going to lose myself here, I met Casey and decided to live my life without hiding who I am."

Vivi said, with a moved expression on her face: "Awww. You and Casey are a dream."

Brittany: "It became harder after that because the day I decided to bring her home for Christmas as my girlfriend, my dad kicked me out of the house. We had this huge argument about how he could be so hypocritical to be part of the same oppressive system that years before, did the same to him when he married mom. A system that still discriminates him no matter how much education he has or who he fell in love with. I think that conversation shocked him because now, 4 years later he has come to terms with accepting my relationship with Casey. He asks here and there how's she doing and stuff like that, but he is not looking forward to our wedding or anything like that... I think the whole situation was hard on him because it brought him to deal with part of his past. As a young black man, he had to overcome a lot of obstacles, especially when he fell in love with mom. Dad is a very smart lawyer but as an African American man in this country, he has gone through a lot of prejudice and life has not been easy on him. I know he comes from a good place. He just doesn't want his only child to struggle like he had too. Plus, he is very stubborn... I am too" she said with pride on her face. Brittany recognized that she was exactly like her father.

Kimberly: "Now I see where you get it from. It must be hard for you to have gone through that experience. I know how close you are with your family."

Brittany: "Yes it was, but I couldn't live a lie. I just couldn't. That's why it bothers me what this guy did to you. Be a man and have ownership of your life."

Kimberly: "I agree. This is exactly what makes me angry. He could have told me he was bi. Then, I would have decided if I wanted to be with him or not. I felt deceived. I was not expecting this at all. Honestly, I knew something was going on, but I thought it was a girl, not a guy."

Vivi: "Would have been better though? Deception is deception."

Kimberly: "Deception is deception, and I could have gotten an STD no matter if it was with a girl or a man. It's about the fact that this is a big lie and, how could he? You know? He knew my ex fiancé left me for another woman. How could you look at my face and be empathetic and do this behind my back?"

Brittany: "The guy is trash. Full trash. You deserve better"

Vivi: "Well, everything is fine and Kimberly, you are a very strong and assertive woman. I know you will overcome this situation in no time."

Kimberly: "If you girls thought I did not get attached easily before, after this one, I will definitely not."

Vivi: "I bet"

Kimberly, while extending her hands to grab Vivi's & Brittany's hands: "Ladies, I appreciate you listening to me. You know I don't like to deal much with feelings, but I wanted to thank you. I also wanted to ask you if you could keep this between us."

Vivi: "Of course"

Brittany: "No word of it"

Kimberly: "Thank you"

R-E-S-P-E-C-T

Pepper was with John on their way home from brunch at a lovely French restaurant in their neighborhood. It was a sunny Sunday and Pepper was happy to finally spend some time with John, since they both had some crazy work hours lately. They were both holding each other by the waist and walking when John said: "Honey, do you think that we can invite my parents for dinner next Sunday? I know my mom is not easy on you, but I would really like to see them."
Pepper was about to say one of her typical sarcastic replies, but since she knew John was having a tough situation at work lately and they were having a nice day out, she decided to bite her tongue and just reply with an: "of course babe". Next Sunday came, and Pepper was feeling she was on her A-game. She had cooked all the recipes of a 4-course meal from scratch. She had asked John his mom's and dad's favorite plates and prepared a menu around it. His parents had finally arrived, and she was giving the last touches to the meal. By the way she was garnishing the plate, you could just tell the type of perfectionist chef she is. John went to open the door and receive his parents. His mom entered the apartment first and look at the surroundings. She had visited before and every single time there was that look of searching for something to disapprove of. Pepper left the Kitchen after cleaning her hands to greet them. Dinner so far had been great, and Pepper thought that this time, she had won over John's mom. She hadn't said any of her catty comments, so maybe she was impressed

with today's dinner. While they were all having the third course plate, John's mom says: "oh, John your dad and I will go to the Cayman Islands in two weeks for 4 days. Can you please take care of the dog while we are there?": John responds "of course mom". Then she replies "Oh, John... Do you remember when you went on vacation there with Katie? What places do you recommend your dad and I to go to?"

And just like that, Pepper's eyes rolled. Of course, the woman had to mention John's ex-girlfriend Katie!

John said: "Mom" to what she immediately replied, "I just want to know what places are good to visit".

John said "Mom, I don't remember. Katie was the one to plan the places that we went, and I cannot recall the names... it was such long time ago"

His mom said "That girl was really lovely. I saw her mom the other day in the supermarket and she told me she got promoted to Director of Communications at your old job."

Pepper just heard enough and murmured to herself "Are you fucking kidding me?" in disbelief of what she heard. John stared at Pepper with a dead serious expression on his face. He was the only one that heard what Pepper said. His parents didn't notice.

Pepper took a deep breath and went through the rest of the dinner. She couldn't wait for this dinner to be over. Once they finished the dinner and they said good bye, Pepper went straight to the kitchen and slammed the almost empty tray against the sink. The tray where she had previously served the salmon lemon risotto with asparagus. A single teardrop fell over her right cheek.

She was furious and hurt. She usually didn't take shit from anybody and had no problem standing up for herself, but this was the feather that broke the camel's back. This time, she also felt angry with John. She couldn't believe he just stood there with a stunned look on his face and didn't say anything to stop it. Pepper also knew she was not going to be able to have a good relationship with John's parents in the future no matter how hard she tried. It also sank in that she was not going to be able to be with a man that wouldn't stand for her in front of his mom. She was furious because she couldn't believe this woman could always find a way to make her feel inferior. John came to the kitchen while Pepper was cleaning visibly angry.

Trying to lighten up the atmosphere, John said: "Well, I guess by now, we are pretty up to date with Katie's life".

Pepper said in a very stern tone: "Like I wanted one"

John: "Honey, you got to understand that I was long time with her and my mom just became close to her and her family."

Pepper: "Excuse me? I have to understand? Are you fucking kidding me! She's the one that needs to understand! I am your girlfriend, not Katie. Get over it! Every single time is the same shit over and over. I heard enough of Katie already!"

John: "But baby"

Pepper: "Baby, nothing. You also stood there and said nothing. Are you ever going to stand up to her? Or, are you going to let her keep treating me like shit?! Your mom doesn't have any type of respect for me or our relationship and it's up to you show her otherewise.

Unless... you also believe this is not going anywhere. Is that the case John? If it is, just don't make me waste my time."

John: "Are you listening to yourself? Of course I see a future with us. You are the woman I love, and the only woman I care about."

Pepper: "Then how can you not stand up to your mom?"

John: "I just ignore her."

Pepper: "I cannot ignore her. Her comments are hurtful, and she always goes out of her way to say comments that are not only inappropriate, but also disrespectful to me as your girlfriend. It took a lot of me not to argue with her today and honestly, I am not taking her punches anymore. Sorry if I don't meet her high standards of wife material but I know who I am. If she doesn't accept it, it's her problem. I have put on my part to try to build a relationship with her, but I am not looking the other way anymore while she stomps over me. I am not allowing it."

John kept quiet...

The next day, John called his mom via FaceTime.

His mom picks up the phone and says: "Hi Johnny. How are you?"

John: "I am good mom. How are you and dad?"

Mom: "We are good. We just came from church."

John: "Mom, I need to talk to you. It's about Patricia."

Mom: "What about her? She seemed upset at the dinner last night."

John: "Mom, like it or not, Patricia (Pepper) is the woman I love with all my heart and you need to RESPECT her. She is not like Katie and I am glad she is not like her. She makes me really happy and I wouldn't change her for anything. I can listen to you, but the decisions for our future are not yours to decide."

After that convo, John continued with a "Is this clear mom?". After a few seconds, he said "And now if you excuse, I will hang up".

Alicia and Vivi met at a fashion show. Alicia was wearing a ruffled Alice + Olivia dress in a gorgeous print, and Vivi was wearing a DVF one off shoulder jumpsuit that fitted her beautifully. While waiting for the show, since they arrived early, they decided to have a drink at the bar of the venue. They seated and ordered 2 champagne glasses.

Alicia: "What are you doing this weekend? Kimberly got promoted and we are planning to go celebrate."
Vivi: "Wait, wait, wait... How do you know about this and I don't?"

Alicia: "Because she told Brittany when they went for lunch last week."

Vivi: "Ramiro is coming to town, so I can go for like an hour or so. Do you know at what time is the celebration?"
Alicia: "Why do you keep doing that to yourself?"
Vivi: "What do you mean?"

Alicia: "Don't play dumb. You know damn well what I am talking about."

Vivi: "Okaaayyy. This went from 0 to 100 pretty quick" while laughing.

Alicia: "Darling, every single time Ramiro comes out of nowhere, you drop everything to dedicate the week to him and give him priority when he doesn't give you a real sense of commitment."

Vivi: "I am just going to go out and have fun. You know, getting laid! I haven't had some in months."

Alicia: "Cut that crap. Every single time is with him... If it was just that, I would tell you: "Go ahead! Have fun!" but the problem is that as soon as he leaves, you are miserable and sad for two whole months. Not only that but you close the door to have any real opportunity to meet a guy because you are waiting for him... Tell me, what are you waiting for? He is not going to show one day and take you like a Prince Charming. You know very well he is going out with women over there and you are here, just mopping and crying"

Vivi: "Harsh much don't you think?"

Alicia: "Sorry darling, but I have been listening to this for 3 years. You needed to hear it sooner or later. This guy only gives you excuses. Don't you think that you deserve better? A guy that is with you for real? A man that wants a future with you? I know you love him, but you need to love yourself more."

Vivi: "You are right. It's not like I want him to marry me tomorrow. Hell, I just want to be in a relationship with someone that loves me and is committed to me... just me"

Alicia: "Exactly! And you deserve that. Stop selling yourself short! You are fabulous, smart, generous, driven, funny and you have a promising career. You deserve a man that doesn't take you for granted and has you in layaway while something better comes along."

Vivi: "I know you are right" while she exhales deeply... "I know you are right"

Alicia: "Darling, I am just telling you because now that I am older, I realized I let good guys pass because I was still hung up on my ex fiancé. Don't want you to go through the same experience."

Vivi met Ramiro a few years back when they were both at a fashion show after party. She was talking with her coworker at the bar and ordering, when they bumped accidentally from behind and turned around. The guy had blonde hair and brown eyes and she was instantly mesmerized. His hair was pulled back in a barely ponytail. He was wearing black ripped jeans, a t-shirt and a leather jacket. She was with a co-worker and he was by himself having a drink.

Vivi: "So sorry! I didn't mean to hit you with my fat ass! So sorry!"

Ramiro: "No worries" while having a small smirk on his lips. He thought she was funny.

After that smirk, Vivi glazed into his eyes while doing small talk. Her coworker saw the whole thing.

Co-worker: "Hey Vivi, I leave you here with ...?" while pointing at him.

Ramiro: "Ramiro" while greeting him with a handshake

Co-worker: "Well Ramiro, take care of my good friend Vivi while I go to congratulate one of the designers of the fashion show we just had today. Is that ok with you?"

Ramiro: "Yes, it's good with me"

Co-worker: "Ok love. See you shortly" she said to Vivi, while touching her shoulder like a see you later way.

Ramiro and Vivi dated briefly since he got an opportunity to move to Los Angeles for an acting job. They kept in contact and every time he would be in town, they would reconnect. Time had passed, and Vivi had developed these strong feelings for this guy but with the years Ramiro had changed. He had become more cocky and flirtatious. Very different from the cool, quiet and sensitive soul Vivi fell in love with.

When he came to NYC, Vivi decided to arm herself with courage and talk to Ramiro about their situation.

Vivi: "Ramiro, you know we have been on and off for a few years now. Do you think we are going to evolve into something else? I know I have brought this topic other times, but I cannot just be attached to a relationship where I don't know if you are 100% there."

Ramiro: "Vivi, you know I am 100% there."

Vivi: "You know what I mean. I'm talking about a real relationship, a commitment. I am not talking about marriage right now, but I want to know if you want to make this work."

Ramiro: "But why don't you let it flow? We work as it is."

Vivi: "Yes Ramiro, but this has been going on for years now and I just need something more. I feel like you are just taking me for granted, even my friends notice. You go out with women in LA, and I understand but I am here just waiting for you and I am tired of that"

Ramiro: "Vivi, Vivi, Vivi"

Vivi: "Don't Vivi me. You know what I am saying is true. You are really comfortable in your situation and it's ok, but don't keep dragging me"

Ramiro: "This feels like an ultimatum and you know I don't like ultimatums."

Vivi: "It's not an ultimatum. I am just tired of our situation. I just don't want to deal with it anymore. It doesn't work for me anymore"

Ramiro: "But you don't understand. I have my career and right now that's the most important to thing to me. I am not ready for something serious at this moment."

Vivi: "And I understand, but I just can't deal with it anymore. I have feelings for you like I haven't had for someone else, but I just can't"

Ramiro: "You are just so stuck in your ways... Well, I guess this is it then"

Vivi: "Yes, I guess this is it" even though she didn't mean that conversation as an ultimatum, but it was very obvious Ramiro was taking her for granted. The way he just dismissed her with that last sentence struck her.

At that exact moment, Vivi felt a strong pain in her heart. A pain that felt like a knife in her soul. She always thought Ramiro was the guy for her, but she also knew she wanted somebody that loved and treated her like she deserved. She knew she wanted someone to have a future with, without excuses. Someone that she did not have to tip toe around when talking about their relationship. Vivi realized that as much as she loved Ramiro, this couldn't go over the love and RESPECT that she had for herself. She wanted her guy to love her and offer her the things she deserved. She didn't need to beg for love.

After many months of dealing with her boss mistreatments, Monica felt so defeated that she called in sick to work just to stay home in bed. She had been going home crying almost every night because even though she had been actively looking for a job, nothing had happened besides a few interviews. That day, when her sister Ana María came from work with Monica's niece Clara, she noticed that Monica was on the sofa wearing her pajamas and watching TV while eating from an ice cream pint.

Monica's sister (Ana María): "And you here so early? Did something happen?"

Monica: "Took a mental day. I did not want to go to work today."

Ana María: "You know what? *Tienes que dejar la mierda. Al carajo tu jefe y deja de tomarte pena.* It's time for you to claim what you deserve at your work or move on."

Monica: "Pero"

Ana María: "But nothing... *No eres ni la primera ni la última que viene a este país y la tratan como mierda. Tu eres muy buena en tu trabajo e inteligente, no dejes que un pinche pendejo te joda la vida. Dáte tu valor y deja la pendejada ya.* Seriously. Stop apologizing and taking it. Nobody that has succeeded in this country, and that came from our background, has not gone through shit like this. You decide if you do something about it or not."

Monica was speechless. Her sister would not usually get into her business. Ana María was her older sister. Their parents had worked hard to bring them to the U.S. They moved when they were young. Ana María got married but after having Clara, she divorced her husband. This was when she and Monica decided to live together.

These words from Ana María sparked a small flame inside of her. She has always admired her sister and looked up to her. She was very strong, didn't let any of her circumstances to get on the way. She was a *purita* Ramírez, just like their mom.

Next day, Monica woke up and went to the office as usual. She noticed a new girl. Her name was Sarah and had less experience in the industry, since she started working a year ago. Monica had already been working 3 years in this company and her reviews were excellent. Her boss told her recently that she will get a raise. However, the raise was pushed back because the company had some setbacks. While at lunch with her friend from work, Monica tells her friend: "Don't you think is weird we are hiring somebody for the same position that I have, when the company is having issues with profit?"

Her work friend Nicole: "Issues with profiting? The company performed really well this last year."

Monica replied: "That's what Frank told me in my last month's review. That's why my raise got pushed back."

Nicole: "Ok. You didn't hear this from me but if I were you, I would start looking for a job. The owners of the company are happy with your work and they were thinking about promoting you to cover another department and not to be under Frank. However, Frank suggested that he could take over that department too and get you promoted to do that, but under his supervision."

Monica: "What?! What a fucker!"

Nicole: "But seriously you cannot say anything. I can get in trouble for telling you."

Monica stayed in awe.

Nicole: "That's why that girl got hired. Because you will have to be dealing with another department too... And I don't pretend you to get you mad, but she is doing slightly less than you. This is the reason I am telling you that you need to get another job."

It was exactly at that point Monica's eyes dilated and she was fuming. The Ramírez part of her that was asleep woke up. Right there, Mónica swore to herself, she was not going to be a pushover anymore. Nobody was going to mess with Monica Ramírez. At least not at work. She was having a sea of emotions running through her body but all she told Nicole was: "Don't worry, I am not saying anything. Thanks for this... I needed it."

When they got back to the office from their break,

Monica, with strong determination, started to write her 2 weeks' notice. She left the date in blank, she printed it and signed it. It was that day, that Monica decided that she would carry herself in a way that would make people RESPECT her. She decided that if she was not treated like this, she was not going to allow this type of people in her life. The rest of the afternoon, she dedicated to follow up with the places that she had interviewed, and had good feedback. She got a response right away from one of the companies, the woman that had interviewed her told her that they hadn't called her because the position was on hold. However, she mentioned to Monica that the budget for that position was just approved and that they would like to meet with her again. Mónica agreed to meet the next day at 8:30am. That day, Monica left just right on time and told her boss that she had a doctor's appointment the next day and that she was coming in about an hour late. The next day, she went to this job's second interview with the company. She went in very determined that she was going to get it and the pay she wanted. A week later, she received the offer and accepted it. She was happy with the money she negotiated. She went to her job, put a date in the 2 weeks' notice letter and scanned She wrote the email addressed to HR and her boss and attached the letter. There was no bigger satisfaction, than when she hit the button to SEND. No more taking crumbs, not more feeling bad about asking for what she deserved, nothing besides R-E-S-P-E-C-T.

RELATIONSHIPS: EFFORT VS. EFFORTLESS

Kimberly & Alicia had gone to Vivi's apartment to pick up clothes that Vivi had separated for them as a gift. She had received them at work and she thought they would look perfect on them. For Kimberly, she got some buttoned shirts that had a very clean design and that she could use at work. For Alicia, she had gotten 2 blouses in very gorgeous prints.

As soon as they walked into Vivi's room, Kimberly said: "What is this? It's an orchid graveyard in here!" There were death orchid arrangements everywhere.

Vivi replied: "I have killed about 20 orchids! 20!!!! Like, who does that?! They are just like my relationships. I keep ruining them all. Why do I keep going for what does not work for me?"

Alicia: "Well, maybe you should stop analyzing it and commit into putting in the work. And if you are not, you just need to move on and not live surrounded by a graveyard of orchid pots... or failed relationships."

Vivi: "Wow, boooom!" as she put her hands on her head and made the sign of an explosion.

Vivi: "You are right, but relationships shouldn't require that much work at the beginning, right? I mean, I understand if you have kids and busy schedules or have been in a relationship long enough that can become a routine... But a boyfriend-girlfriend relationship shouldn't, right?"

Alicia: "It all depends on the work that you want to put into it and if that person is worth it. Plus, remember every single relationship is different. Friendship, lovers, family... all of them. Even co workers. Look at the relationship I have with my patients. Believe me, pregnant women are not easy. The relationship we have, and every caring detail not only makes them come back, but also recommend me to other patients."

Kimberly: "On my opinion, relationships are not fifty-fifty all the time. Some days relationships are eighty-twenty. You need to make sure it's not one hundred on your end and zero on the other person. To have a relationship, you need two people on it. One person cannot do all the work... Life is a balance, you know?"

Vivi: "Thank you both. I know you girls are right. Thanks for your words of wisdom."

Later that week, Vivi received an arrangement of flowers to her apartment. These were white orchids from her friend Kimberly.

The note said: Are you ready to put in the work? I believe in you.

XOX,

Kimberly

Kimberly was not much about feelings, but she always knew how to come through as a friend when you needed her.

Vivi not only realized that she had to put effort taking care of her orchid, but also put effort in the relationship she had with herself. She needed to take care and be gentle with her heart. Something that she too, hadn't taken care of...

HOW DO WE SEE OURSELVES VS. HOW OTHER PEOPLE SEE US?

Pepper went out with Vivi, Kimberly, Brittany and Brittany's girlfriend Casey. It was Friday night, and they went out dancing to a gay club in West Village. They hadn't gone out dancing in a long time, but this was Kimberly's birthday and she wanted to do something different. All ladies wore wigs and they went bar hopping. In each bar, they would exchange their wigs. They were having a lot of fun. All had quite a few drinks, but Kimberly had the most. Pepper was dancing with a guy she bumped into. She knew him. They had worked together in the past while she worked as a roast chef. He was also at a birthday party, his cousin's. Toward the end of the night when all of them were ranging between tipsy to practically wasted, Vivi decided that it was time to go home. Since she hadn't found Pepper inside the club, she went outside to look for her and tell her it was time to go. She went out the door when she found out Pepper out of the club making out with the guy she was dancing all night. She was half wearing her long blonde hair wig.

Vivi yelled at her: "Pepper! We need to go!"

Pepper: "No, but I want to stay. I am having fun."

Vivi: "No, we need to go... Now!" and she went and

grabbed her by the arm.

Guy from the club: "Leave her with me. She wants to stay."

Vivi went all Puerto Rican on him: "*Mira mijo*, my friend has to go so let her go. Ok? Plus, she has a boyfriend so leave her alone ¡*No jodas más*!" while she gave him total neck and index finger move.

Pepper: "Ooooohhh. Vivi is angryyyy."

Vivi: "Stop it Pepper. You are making a fool of yourself. Let's go."

Pepper left the guy and went with her.

Vivi: "I will put you in a cab and text John."

Pepper: "Don't tell John. I love John, but I hate his mom."

Vivi: "If you love John, why were you kissing a stranger?"

Pepper: "It was the wiiiigg."

Vivi: "Oh, so it was the wig then?"

Pepper kept quiet. Vivi put Pepper in an Uber while texting John to give him the heads up that she had a few too many and if he could be alert when she arrived. She sent him the screen shot of the Uber ride. This was all happening while Casey and Brittany did the same for Kimberly. Vivi took a taxi herself, but by the time she was getting home, she was drunk too. She went to the 24-hour open pizza place next to her apartment building and bought one slice to take home. When opening the door, she was already crying because she was emotional about the fact that her love life had been a disaster. She was missing Ramiro and couldn't understand why she couldn't find a good man that she loved, who loved her back. When she opened the door of her apartment, her roommate Adam came out of his bedroom and asked her "are you ok?"

Vivi answered: "No" and went full mood crying.

Vivi: "I just don't get it. Why? Why does my love life sucks? Why can't I find the right guy for me?" She kept crying. "I just don't get it. I am not a bad person"

Adam was like her younger brother. All he could say was: "Don't worry Vivi. Dating in New York is hard. Don't think it's you, it's not."

Vivi went to her room and fell asleep with her clothes on next to the pizza slice she had bought.

The next day she woke up and took a shower. She texted Pepper: We need to talk. Let's grab brunch.

Pepper replied: Ok. Is it about last night?

Vivi texted: Yes. Let's do brunch in Yuca.

This was a Latin cuisine restaurant/bar. They needed something heavy to eat.

Pepper replied: Ok. It's going to take me like a 1 ½ hour to get ready and arrive. See you at 12:30pm.

Pepper arrived at the restaurant wearing her black shades, a vintage Levi's t-shirt and her Rag & Bone jeans. They were both hungover, so they drank their water glasses quickly. They also both asked for coffee. Pepper ordered an americano and Vivi ordered a black coffee.

Vivi: "So, do you remember what happened last night? We were all drunk, but you and Kimberly were wasted. We had to put you in an Uber and send you home."

Pepper: "Yeah, I barely remember. John told me this morning that you texted him last night and he was waiting up by the window."

Vivi: "Awww... And talking about John, what was last night all about?

Pepper: "What do you mean? Are you talking about my ex co-worker?"

Vivi: "Of course I am referring to the guy! I mean, what's the deal?"

Pepper: "I remember we made out... I guess it was the wig. She made me do it" and laughed. She was not a jokester, but she knew Vivi was, so she was trying to lighten up the mood.

Vivi: "I am not going to judge you, but I am giving you an advice. You have a good man. Don't do anything stupid. If you are not happy with him, leave him, but don't hurt him or yourself."

Pepper: "I am happy with him. I love him."

Vivi: "Then, why are you self-sabotaging the relationship with the first guy that is good to you? Aren't you tired of listening to us complaining about how hard dating is? All the commitment foe, the cheaters, the assholes out there? Didn't you have enough with Ricky, Christian & Daniel? After what happened to Kimberly? Again, I am not going to judge but as your friend, I have to tell you some truth. Last night...it was not the alcohol, it was you sabotaging yourself and I am not going to allow it. You play all tough and everything but it's ok to be vulnerable. I know you are scared to get hurt again, but you should give yourself a chance to be happy. John seems like he really loves and cares for you. Why jeopardize your happiness because you are scared? Who cares if his mom doesn't like you! He likes you and that's all that matters."

Pepper: "I know. I have never cared about what people thought of me and would send them to screw themselves in no time. I don't even know why I am acting this way."

Vivi: "Maybe because you care about him and you want things to go well? All I am saying is that you have something good. You are an adult, and you can do with your life whatever you want. I am here to support you, however, I am going to be honest with you and let you know what I think."

Pepper: "Sounds fair"

There was a quick awkward silence between them and Vivi decided to change the conversation.

Vivi: "Anyways, want to know what I did last night? Went home crying like a freaking idiot and poor Adam went out thinking something happened to me."

Pepper: "But did something happen to you on your way home?"

Vivi: "Nothing happened besides that my love life sucks! Not only that, but ended up falling asleep next to my freaking slice of pizza! Didn't eat it, but just slept next to it! This morning I tossed it to the garbage... Well, at least I didn't eat it and gain the weight." and started laughing.

Pepper: "You wasted pizza? That's a capital sin."

Vivi: "Yes, for you! You are skinny and can eat everything you want. As I get older, this metabolism is not getting any faster. I look at a freaking donut and gain weight!"

Pepper: "Oh, please." and laughed.

Vivi: "Seriously! And God forbid I gain a little bit of weight. Last time I went home to visit was a torture. I had gained 5 pounds and my cousin told me "Watch out! You haven't had kids and are already bloated." Even my aunt grabbed me by the arm while I was eating and told me: "You look beautiful but *estás gorditaaaa*. Which means fat!"

Pepper: "Oh, please. You are exaggerating."

Vivi: "I swear I am not! You talk about John's mom but at least you have a relationship. In our Latin culture, we get the saying: "Oh, no boyfriend yet? Then, if you find a boyfriend, the question is: when are you getting married? If you get married, the question is: when will you are having kids? You can never please anyone."

 "I started to respond that I was going to be a cat lady in my last visit back home and people started: No, how come? while staring at you with a pity look in their eyes."

Pepper: "I cannot believe you."

Vivi: "I am serious, and that's not even the worst part. The worst part is that sometimes you get told you are being too picky and not to worry that you will find a guy. Not a good man or someone that loves you, but a guy! Like I waited this long just to find any guy!"

Pepper: "But don't get angry. It seems like it's a sensitive subject to you."

Vivi: "Of course it is! Because it's every single visit, same set of questions. Then, come the looks like if something is wrong with you."

Pepper: "You know there's nothing wrong with you. You might be a little bit crazy but it's good crazy." Laughs and continues "Now I tell YOU, does it matter what other people think?"

On Vivi's taxi ride home, she felt good about her conversation with Pepper. She realized that her friends saw her faults and her strengths.

After arriving home, she found a note from Adam on the fridge that read:

You are an amazing girl and any guy that cannot appreciate or see that, is not worthy of you. You will find a great man. I promise you will.

She read the note and felt happier. It was not about seeing ourselves through the eyes of other people. Instead, it was about finding a balance between looking at our faults and looking ourselves through the eyes of the people that matter, the ones that love us. Vivi knew that even if she hadn't found the "love of her life", she had found good friendships and a family that loved her for who she was... a *Gracious Hot Mess*.

BALANCING FAMILY & CAREER: *THE LITTLE GUIDE FOR THE SINGLE & WORKAHOLIC*

Here I am. I just left my dad's funeral and I am writing because it's the best thing I can do to pour out my feelings at 4 in the morning. His death was something that nobody saw coming. As any seventy-two-year-old, he was what you would consider an elderly person however, he would not behave like one. He was full of life and with a joke on his lips ready to come out when needed, he was the happiness of the family. My dad was not the typical dad. He would drop and pick up us from school. He was the only dad in a group of a bunch of moms at every parent-teacher meeting. Always supportive, even when I decided to leave Engineering school for a career in fashion, and later had to move away from the family to pursue it. When he was mad, he used to tell me comments like "I am not an ATM" and "What are you going to do when I die?". These words made me roll my eyes at that moment, but now resonate strongly in my head. Having a "good job" in fashion (if there's such a thing) that pays the bills and following my passion, is thanks to my father for being the first person that believed in me.

As we move to a more stable career path and our life becomes busy with our daily routines, it's hard not to get cluttered with the to do lists that bring us nowhere when we are looking into the bigger picture. It's in these kind of moments that we get hit by walls that force us to make reality checks on what's really important in life. I am not saying to quit your job and start a new life tomorrow free of worries and responsibilities. However, it's important to pay attention to every single detail. Even when I was pretty good at coming home 2-3 times a year, and had been there when my parents got sick or had a surgery, I realized today I've missed a lot of small happy moments that were the ones that filled most of the last 7 years of my dad's life. It was a hard reality that I had to face, as the pictures were projecting on the tv next to his body at the chapel, and I could barely find myself in a few of them. Nowadays, there's a lot of ways to communicate and even though I spoke with my dad regularly, it's hard to avoid the feeling that I still could have done more. Sometimes it feels that to achieve your goals, you must make sacrifices, but we don't know the cost of those sacrifices. We do small trades here and there because we think there's always a tomorrow, but there are days that the tomorrow becomes today, and those small trades had a greater cost that we could ever imagine.

That's why I recommend to:

1.) *Create routines or rituals with your parents* - This applies to when you are away, as well as when you are close by. If you only speak with them even once a week, try to Skype or FaceTime with them. Try to keep that visual connection. Even if you do not think so, it makes a big difference. When you go to see them, you can plan activities together, like trying a new restaurant or visiting a new coffee shop, that keeps both looking foward for your next fun adventure. Not that we don't love staying home with the parents, but this will help create a much deeper bond and excitement.

2.) *Connect your parents with your world* -
Sometimes, we disregard this by saying that our parents are not tech savvy and we often underestimate them. Have a WhatsApp group with your family, open a Facebook account for your mom, share recipes or funny videos and memes with your parents.

3.) *The beauty is in the little details* –
The reason that you are away is no excuse to forget about the small details. It's a special holiday and you cannot visit, there's no reason to forget about it or not do something special for our loved ones. A call is ok, but it says way more if you can prepare a small detail. Nowadays, there are plenty of places that can deliver small gifts and they don't cost too much. Chocolate covered strawberries, flowers, postal cards, even a lunch or dessert delivery... there are no reasons to not plan something special with today's technology. Remember,

relationships take work and the one we have with our family is the most important.

Treat every day like it's the last. It's okay if we don't agree with our family in everything and to have disagreements, but it's very important not to be angry for long time. If you have an argument in a call, try to solve that issue on the same call. Regret is one of the worst feelings you can have, so think: Is it really worth it? Don't sweat the small stuff and don't lose perspective of what's really important in life.

Follow the author:
@melissa_trendalert (Instagram) & @meli_trendalert (Twitter)

Follow the book:
@AGraciousHotMess (Instagram), A Gracious Hot Mess Page
(Facebook) & @GraciousHot (Twitter)

CPSIA information can be obtained
at www.ICGtesting.com
Printed in the USA
BVHW041114180420
577880BV00014B/2761